Scra e

Praise for Dave Lewis's poetry:

"The poems are sharp, clear, and confident. He has a clarity only a real poet possesses."
- *Brian Patten*

"An engaging and diverse range of poems, well-crafted and driven by theme and form. The subjects are varied, but this confident poet succeeds in melding them into a coherent and rewarding collection."
- *David J Costello*

"Dave Lewis is a true Welsh poet of the Valleys."
- *Catrin Collier*

"His poetry is honest and direct. Each word is effective. Each word is easily understood. Unlike so many others today, he writes from the heart and soul, from raw emotion; he has drawn on his wide-ranging knowledge and experience to evolve a style, an elevated poetic diction, which eschews artifice and ornate language."
- ***John Evans***

"Dave Lewis's work possesses an energy and freshness that lifts his imagery and empathy way above the work of many less ambitious poets."
- *Sally Spedding*

"The humour is dark, the love is bright, the poetry is touching, taunting, spewing, galling, tender."
- *Eloise Williams*

"The poems are deceptively complex... seemingly easily accessible but with deeper reading wrought with a covert enigmatic depth that remains unresolved."
- *Mike McNamara*

"Dave Lewis is a storyteller: sharply observant, witty and whimsical."
- *Kathy Miles*

"The stark reality Mr Lewis painted left me breathless. Readers will ride a rollercoaster of rich language, clever insights and creativity."
- *Jolen Whitworth*

"If Dave Lewis's work doesn't make you feel, then you might as well give up on this poetry lark… because that's what he does best. Make you feel!"
- *Agnes Meadows*

"His free-flowing verse makes him a Welsh son of the Beats."
- *Mike Jenkins*

"A compassionate poet of emotion and sensitivity; his use of pared down concise language and short simple forms is very successful."
- *Gillian Drake*

"Dave Lewis is a unique voice in the poetry world."
- *Moira Andrew*

"An outcry and reassertion of the true feelings of the individual, unhidden, unashamed and fiercely assertive of the beat that runs through us all."
- *Mick Evans*

Scratching The Surface

Poems

Dave Lewis

Publish & Print
www.publishandprint.co.uk

ISBN: 9781693570933

Published by www.publishandprint.co.uk

Special thanks to Brian Patten, David J Costello, Sally Spedding and Catrin Collier for their wonderful comments and support

Front cover photo: Craig Adderley
Back cover photo: Jake Melara
Back cover author photograph: Dave Jones

Some of these poems have been published in: Frogpond Journal, Modern Haiku, Nine Muses Poetry and Under the Basho

'Follow your inner moonlight; don't hide the madness.'
- *Allen Ginsberg*

CONTENTS

Rivers	1
You and I	7
River Wye Weekend	8
Stranger in a Strange Land	9
Egypt	10
Autumn Garden	12
Pills	13
You sweep all the darkness away	14
Half Empty Bed	15
Scratching The Surface	16
You came early	17
Dislodged Stone	18
Foreigner	20
A Red Sighting	21
March, 2019	22
A Dream of Gawain	23
Those were different times	24
I Miss You	26
Isolation	29
Cardiff	30
Turkish Chip Shop	32
Poured People	33
Gentrification	35
For David Neville	36
Christmas Dad	38

We're driving up the Skeleton Coast	39
When an 18hr train ride became 23	40
From Etosha to Okavango	42
Over the Cwm	43
Sunset over Penally	44
Haiku	45
Tết	46
Somewhere near Barcelona	47
Out of the Depth	48
Belle de Jour	50
Trivial things	51
Dancer	52
Porphyra	53
Bebe the Pomeranian made it to Lifeboat 7	54
Far from Plain Jayne	56
Outlaw	57
European Tinder	59
Blood River	60
Wet morning	61
Sarah	62
Angelystor	64
Spaceman	65
Hunchback	67
Flame retardant	68
The cup of the world	69
Cabinda	70

Good Day 71

Laika 73

Alois 74

Goshawk 75

Blade 76

Pure Heart 77

Haiku 79

Notes 81

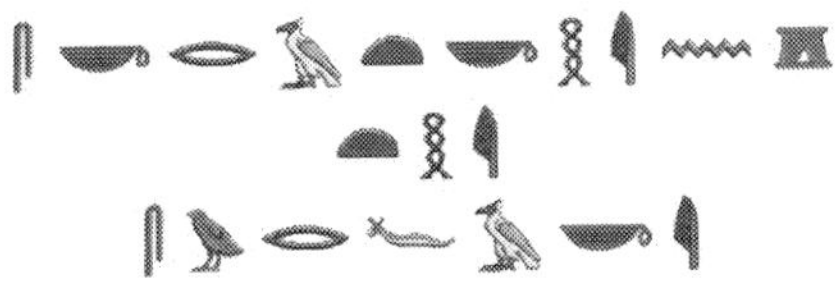

Rivers

I dreamed I was a butterfly, hovering around the room.
Blissful in my ignorance I gaze into your eyes,
but suddenly I'm falling,
down, down, down I go,
back to the cave of darkness
where all I am I am.

Waking in a curious state,
I see you circumnavigate,
self medicate, reverberate,
tessellate, infiltrate,
mutate and advocate…

Remember, this ain't no Mesopotamia,
more like a Netflix septicaemia.
For the more you learn
the less you'll leave,
like a splinter in the mind
your room number already assigned,
you can't breakout of your habitat
but don't forget Winston and his rats.

Above the city streets a fog is forming around the houses.
Across the river we see the smoke rise from the fires.
I feel your arms wrap around me now,
'Let's take a rest from genocide,' you say.
You lick your lips, all southern fried,
'Why don't we take a trip to the countryside?'
Up, up, up we go,
down, down, down we go.

I see the god of dreams,
he's holding out his hand
and in his palm he has two tempting sweets
that he's taken from the cookie jar,
for you to decide if it's au revoir or the oyster bar.

You show me the policewoman
who looks after you and me.
With her guns and Tasers she's our safety net,
with her shapely neck and Internet,
bayonet, dragnet, brunette…
we're intoxicated by reality.

Then I see a man walking up our garden path,
getting nearer all the time.
And as he starts to fade away
he's whispering, 'Closer, closer, closer.'
Up, up, up he goes,
down, down, down he goes.
Climbing the stairs,
shooting the rapids,
playing musical chairs
with stars and snakes
through little earthquakes
and fifty-fifty sweepstakes.

'Aren't you lucky?' cries Hobson, as you lead your nag away.
'But ask yourself, is he sweating on Groundhog Day?'

For sedate is just another name for checkmate,
and when you finally *say hello to your little friend*,
kick the habit,
            kill the rootkit
                        and mend…

Over your shoulder you'll see
the evil demon running up the hill
'the sky, the earth, the colours, shapes and sounds'
and all that appears to be free
so regurgitate your poison pill
you rake, you libertine, you hare and hounds,
you Christmas tree, master key and wannabe.

Upside down and back to front, in-between the smokescreen

when you hear the organ play a tune, ascending and descending keys,
you're submarine and trampoline,
you better check you're still plugged into
the experience machine.

And the sheikh says you look good in your suicide vest.
'Best get it on camera, you know it's for the best!'

'Let them eat cake!' she cries.
'Time for a tea break!' Sanson lies.

'Kill all the black cats!' says Gregory Four.
'Here comes the plague onto the dance floor.'

'I nominate my good friend Adolf Hitler.'
'He's surely not as bad as Jack the Ripper?'

'Muzzle that bitch, put a spike in her tongue.'
'Chop down the ladder, rung by rung.'

'And don't forget the unsinkable,
satanic, Britannic, volcanic, nirvanic, Titanic
that tried to bring the cave dwellers out of the cave and into the sunlight.

The battle has begun; they've taken over the press,
censoring men for peace, click, click, click,
tap, tap, tap.
They give you a cause to hang your flag on
they give you a wall to sit cross-legged upon
they offer you a Babylon, if you kill Genghis Khan
they make believe you're alpha plus
but behind your back they're laughing at you - epsilon.

And when the day is done
and you've finished the bull run
you'll discover that the bricks they gave you

are devoid of spray gun poetry
they've thrown out your dreams
topped up God's debris.
And that someone has
one-by-one, silenced everyone
like a hit and run, aircraft gun.

Maybe in a far-off place, far from the reach of her media-savvy electronic tentacles
a young man stretches his arms above his head as he walks out from a dense forest next to a clear mountain lake.

Is that the moon?
The moon!

And he might try to visit them
to search for murmurations, Dalmatians, work stations.
He'll try to reconnect, with retrospect,
project hen-pecked, the greenhouse effect and intellect.

Amongst populist museum pieces moulded in wax
he'll spin the wheel, bet on parallax.
The truth was a lie,
the lie was a man, the man was a cow, the cow was grass
soft beneath your calloused bare feet,
inhaling the middle-class, atomic mass, nerve gas,
the ultimate deceit, mincemeat, time sheet,
checking your boarding pass
through the looking glass.

Silenced by a click of the mouse
where their clearing house becomes your slaughterhouse,
jailhouse, whorehouse,
dormouse and sucking louse.
But never a lighthouse –
think to blink to drink to stink.
Stink to kink to hoodwink to lip sync.

I want to be with my children,
I want my mind to be cured.
I don't want to be beaten, or cut or ridiculed.
I want things to be fair.

Starting with a trickle the water it grows and grows
until soon you'll be experiencing a natural juxtapose.
The pressure will increase like the Wailing Wall,
they'll change the protocol during a conference call
and sacrifice your mind like a waterfall.
Rough rocks, sly as a fox, tumbling liquid in the press box,
Goldilocks at the ballot box, mid course aftershocks.
Then she meanders; we think it's going to be alright
until you see a brake light on your birth right,
dynamite, hermaphrodite, phagocytes on your opening night.
And finally a slow bend is a welcome change
from the rifle range stock exchange.

Parasitic off our body heat
sucking out obsolete,
offer a trick or a treat,
a window seat, a regular drumbeat
in exchange for a deleted tweet
that used to be found somewhere down on Fleet Street.

And so butterfly, with your wing beat so slow
now is the time you need to make your choice.
Rainbow or skid row?
Game show or polio?
Afterglow or quid pro quo?

For we are losing ground on the merry-go-round
and need to turn around, tune in to ultrasound
to make it all work out OK.

Close your eyes and feel the mist roll in off the sea.
Peel off the layers you devotee
and exult in your time

with your partners in crime
as acorns grow
like an embryo.

As an eagle flies across the sky
reach out your hand and smile
draw your masterpiece and ossify
catch memories to stockpile
for your forever mind's eye.

You and I

You're an ocean wave, when I'm a grain of sand.
You're a skyscraper, when I'm a pane of glass.
You're a mountaintop, when I'm a flake of snow.
You're an open road, when I'm a car that goes.
You're a waterfall, when I'm a drop of rain.
You're a blue, blue sky, when I'm an aeroplane.

You're a rainforest, when I'm a monkey's cry.
You're a stadium, when I'm a drunk barfly.
You're a warm blanket, when I'm icy cold.
You're a clear lake, when I'm offered gold.
You're a spinning world, when I'm a photograph.
You're a savannah, when I'm a small giraffe.

And when I'm lost in the desert you'll kiss me with wine,
and when I'm drowning in sadness you'll be my sunshine smile.

River Wye Weekend

You came in a beat up old blue Landie
with tales of sleeping giants on your lips.
It was your first night in the cottage
when the Wye was skipping over stones,
dividing the spiked water milfoil
with sacred Pumlumon Fawr sunk into the sunset.

We watched a heron draggle
in and out of the water crowfoot beds,
trusted we'd see muntjac or wild boar tomorrow.
Look, there's a kingfisher, jewelled above the otter's holt
and later a dipper, teeter-totter,
near the yellow-cress.

Watching frogs collared by ripples
we wish for a grass snake or polecat.
Skipping past horse-tail and great willowherb
you trace the sand martins with your miniature fingertips
while I collect peppery chives from the bedrock
and turn my once carefree soul to my stomach.

Stranger in a Strange Land

Some mentioned chromosomes, others the devil,
but blood is thicker than water
and layers are meant to be peeled.
Your dad said, 'Watch that boy, he'll be Prime Minister one day!'
You took off your impish grin, like lipstick.
After watching Dennis Hopper you rode a Harley across Route 66,
lived in a tepee down west Wales for five years.
Mam told us about you working on a kibbutz in Israel,
searching for your own Jerusalem.
As a transient phenotype we feared for your safety
when the news about Nilson came on the TV.
Then Gillian inherited the millions,
the London Monopoly game, hotel chain, life never the same,
while all you got was a messy separation,
from a witch who ran the cat sanctuary.
Last time I saw you? Our auntie's funeral.
A fading portrait, a hippy Marilyn,
no clue you were bored with your denomination.
Then silence for years, like families do,
until a butterfly smoking on social media.
I see the madness now, cocooned within the screen,
a sense of entitlement, betrayal, a sliding façade.
Cousin Ceri said you'd divorced your gender,
sloughed the brand. Like a suicide your clothes on the beach,
a seventy-year old epicene, identity theft, craving *grok*.
You leave me messages about granddad's old miners lamp
but I have no idea about that.
All I do know is that we're all looking to cut free of some things,
those membranes and skins, integuments and films,
but some of us are far too afraid of the blade.

Egypt

It slinks out of a pile of dusty old photographs
like a sagging windsock, *per ardua*
on a runway in Aden.

The face smiling back at me from the grave
"brown as a berry, tough as a nut",
I'll put it in the drawer with your medal.

Out the window grey and white cumulus
form a Venn diagram with the sun
and then get scribbled over by a local raptor.

You saw vultures over Benghazi and Cairo,
glimpsed giant cat-like heads at dawn,
killed your own snakes before breakfast,

swam in that shipping lane
all powerful and fertile as fields,
passed cigarettes around.

At home you loved the green forests of oak,
cold streams in the summer,
the copper paths of beeched autumns.

Never talked much about firefights
or the heads they cut off with the wires
they raised from Empire's telegraph poles

but I knew enough I guess
even on the day you shut down
with the thickness in your lungs.

Walking at night beneath the stars
I sometimes remember you again
- all those moments lost in tears.

Silver halide features fading in time
I sit down, breathe deeply and continue
to run rough fingers through love.

Autumn Garden

They always cleared the garden together,
him digging new potatoes from their trenches,
her pruning the blooming blackcurrant bushes.
But each year it got harder, some forgotten task,
another tomato plant discarded in the compost.
Then all too soon it became too much.
She paid the young lad from next door
to dig the bean row, build a wooden decking
and eventually lay cold grey slabs upon the lawn.
It's easier this way, she would usually say,
to anyone who'd listen, on the slow bus into town
on a Friday afternoon when she'd struggle with the shopping
before her favourite TV programmes came on.
Repeats and re-runs of old comedies
on digital channels named after her beloved son.
Sometimes she turns to ask him…
but all she hears is the ticking of the clock
so she totters to the kitchen instead.
A nice cup of tea is what she needs.

Pills

It's not like I want to be one of the selective six million.
It's not like I had a choice, you tell me
over sedate teacups in the second-hand bookshop.
Your serotonin eyes yo-yo to a full moon
and your blood tattoos become visible, like a Dylan print
about trains or an old map maker's stained parchment,
as the long sleeves ride up on your pretty flower dress
to expose you to this desiccated world like a tide rushing out.
Then you calmly tell me that you used to see
so many, very different versions of the sky,
where devils and dragons threw fire at the stars
but now all you see is a fog and a glue and a misty grin,
washed out by those asparagus-coloured pills
and a small light, less ordinary and constant
and sometimes you wish for the monsters to return
so you'll know you're alive one more time
but you're afraid of the doorbell and the pavement
and those people who walk down the street,
'cos they might see you for what you really are.

You sweep all the darkness away

You stand beside me
and sweep all the darkness away.
You say business is good
and I'm good for business.
You're Bowie-eyed, honey-haired,
seeking out the sadness in summer,
munching on the mud of despair,
absorbing the black and white Tsunami
as the wind rushes over the foam
and blood is broadcast into the home,
you are the neap tide of reason,
the calming of my storm,
the blinking of my eyes
and the open palms
of peace of mind.

Half Empty Bed

When the moment of maybe metamorphoses to must
my mood loses mellow, gains momentum.
Like ECG spikes before a stock market correction
oh those words dug deep
wasn't expecting that
from you,
a rare moment that alarms like morning.
Let's put it off,
let's pretend it won't ever happen.
So mashed, petrified passion assassin.
I can understand why some follow into the depths
or get wizards etched on arms,
fight with the live ones,
inject poison
or just top up with Citalopram on a regular basis,
echo prescription.

Maybe it'll be different this time?
It wasn't good the first time that's for sure,
you were left swimming in circles
drowning more like
in a half empty bed.
While that life that was still ticking
ticked-tocked,
ticked-tocked.
'I been here before.'
Like a beautiful sunset it was very welcoming,
conventional,
'cos believing in lies
is always acceptable.

Scratching The Surface

Skimming like dolphins down the Newquay road in a lime-green VW van,
bronzed arm tapping out tunes on the sunset metal of a summer night.
Slept on the beach with the *Cool* Mwynt *Breeze* and that girl covered in beads from Laugharne Castle.
We'd stopped off at Brown's, sat in the corner, 'neath the picture – you a coffee in your shaking hand, me all cryptic and staring.
We were stocking up tinnies after that Three Cliffs binge but to be honest we'd hardly scratched the surface.
She told us she was hitching so we showed her the way, our clocks abandoned months previous.
'Where you boys going?' she floated, and really dug it when we shrugged our shoulders.
Between *Tangled Up In Blue* and *Dancing Barefoot* I mumbled something about ancients forests and the Knights of the Round Table.
She was much younger than us, looked like a surfer who'd lost her wave, but through the rags and the rainbows we had a good feeling – she topped up our freedom at no cost to us.
And as the stars came out we swore we were in Marin, always dreaming of the greener grass – the cafés in Tangier, the vibe in Unawatuna, the rooftops of Stone Town and that cottage tucked away in the palms on Tiwi.
We took it in turns, to collect her raindrops, the story was a sad but familiar one.
She said, 'The beauty of the places is the globe spinning round, getting off the ride is never an option.'
I think we dropped her at Dale after too much tequila, and you still singing that we're only just starting to scratch the surface.

you came early

There was no water to surf in on, just a vacuum of space.
You screamed like a Mexican torture victim as we smiled -
a blast into the future, trumpeted entrance
as Tom Petty sang about the great wide open.
And the crowd wanted to copy your tape,
the friends and the friends of friends,
'What's this track?' asked the anaesthetist,
the womb party in full swing.
The African slicer thought I was a doctor,
apprehensive for lawsuits as they are now,
then sighing relief when Pat laughed,
'No mun, zoology I think it was, and then P.E.,
he's just curious love.'
And then they carted you off to give steroids
like a miniature Schwarzenegger,
something about your lungs - like we were worried!
Then for a week or so they told us you'd be fine
even though Sue already knew how the dream ended.
I remember you curling a finger,
like a fern frond with prehistoric purpose
in your sterile spaceship suspended in time.
A week later we held you, like a doll they all said,
your room overgrown with fresh flowers.

Dislodged Stone

Moonlight collecting in the dimples of your back,
a long-eared owl bleats her disapproval.
My blanket and my beer, warm and cool,
like your breasts after the river.
When I fell you laughed,
cried, 'Do it again!'
Then held out your hand
and stripped me off
with forceful, vanilla-sweet kisses.
Woke up that night to soft footsteps,
'A deer?' you begged.
'A fox more like.'
But all I saw was mute shadows
for the whole world ended at your lips
and your red hair tumbling down –
an Ellen Terry portrait,
I used to tease you in the museum
while our baby sucked the life out of you.

*

Now I'm drinking on the decking,
in the hottest summer since.
Wielding a screwdriver to a photo frame
an old wedding shot is sacrificed
for our prom queen daughter.
I guess that ancient forest is overgrown now,
the path submerged in malignant bracken –
I bet even the ghosts have pulled up their roots.
So we two sleep out behind the kitchen,
sketched outlines against a bat-brown sky.
Then out of the darkness of my memories

I see an angel rise and stretch,
'Dad, I'm going to bed now.
This is such a waste of time.'
'Oh, just a minute longer babe.
The moon's just hidden behind those clouds…'
Then suddenly you've broke free again
and I smile when we hug and watch you glistening up there.

Foreigner

I'm surprised how quickly sorrow can come
when the holly is pregnant with berries
or when I realise the birds have all flown.
It is then that I wish to be a farmer,
leaning on gates, gabbing with a friend
about halos round the moon
or the thickness of acorns
in this warmer November.
And walking the mountains
I'd pause at the path that stretches before me
like steam from a simmering black pot
on a campfire deep in the woods.

And in this alien place I struggle
with my hands that are bruised with time
shuffling the dirty coins
towards the girl at the counter
as she prepares a beef sandwich
annoyed at this old man
who is keeping her from what she calls music
on her iPhone all shiny and new.
Seems I'm a foreigner in my own world,
neither one thing or the other
in limbo like a squirrel
with too many nuts to bury.

A Red Sighting

deer drinking in a sun-soft clearing
my hand on the bark of an oak
open-beaked jay, like a frightened child, afraid to speak
snouts raining, drizzle river
grasshopper symphony, swallowing my lungs
damselfly dart, a flash of rainbow trout
your ears snapped to my yawn
sternum-thundering heart
flitter haunch, tremble loins
sweat drips upon bluebell leaves
snapped twig like an eagle wing clap
lope lightning, cocoa gone green woods
between silence and breath

March, 2019

The blueness of his eyes is just a vague memory now,
a single day like *The Hundred Years War.*
You do the washing up, shower and sit,
watch the sparrows in the birdbath,
read a book, tidy drawers again.
Catch the bus to fetch a paper,
the one he always used to buy.
You put your slippers on,
then your shoes away,
until it's shopping day.

Now it's time to check the fridge,
then the TV page in your terraced cage.
You tell me about the garden
and all the weeds that are there,
then you brush your hair,
like someone cares.
You mention the bank statement,
how it's late this month,
then you wash your cup
and fill the kettle up.

A Dream of Gawain

If you should find yourself lost among the lily ponds of Bosherston, contemplating the magic of those Penrose stairs, take some time to breathe the same freshwater air that tiptoed through the lungs of the hermit Saint Govan one thousand and a half years ago. And perhaps slowly trace the clouds with fairy-tale cartography, gaze forever upon the antique summer sun and picture, secreted in this prehistoric fissure, King Arthur's nephew, in the twilight of his years, having made his peace with the Green Knight, dodging pirates, eating fish and drinking from the holy well. Listen for his cries, bobbing on the wind like a Manx Shearwater or a Chough, then place your hands upon the stone shadows and make a wish. Can you hear a whinny, swirling through the toothy marram and settling on your brine-soaked lips? Maybe it's the ghost of Sir Gawain's heroic white horse, Gringolet, with red ears, *keincaled*. And while the old man is mourning for the death of his steed in combat, imagine him ringing that silver bell, pure as the maidens of youth. Later, after watching shooting stars on Broad Haven beach I dreamt of angels encasing, in a giant whelk of stone, the Bell Rock, now tolling louder than thunder and as the breakers tattoo legends into the jagged coastline's edge I wake amongst a bed of thrift to the distant shimmer of a whale's song.

Those were different times

those were different places.
We were happy people
watching crabapple blossom
floating on the breeze,
you in your white cotton dress,
me picking poppies.
And there were other smiling things,
gold under chins -
swapping buttercups,
we were hopscotch lovers
beneath a candelabra of horse chestnut.

And we were mad
and we were raging,
kissing the belonging night
glass to glass,
lip to lip.

I want you to forgive everything
so I can sleep at night,
not in this parallel universe
where you are
not quite so beautiful,
a little imperfect,
rough around the edges,
not so overflowing with love,
pure love
but back in those days
when you cooked laverbread laced with olive oil,
lemon juice and oatmeal
fried on buttered toast.

See the martins nesting below the eaves,
at times like these
I can see your wings
and my chisel chin on your snow white breast,
Alpha plus,
the two of us,
no scars, no hurts,
no cuts that keep bleeding,
no rain on me,
no rain on you,
echo me,
smash the mirrors,
I'll use your eyes instead.

Then thirty years imploded
into haziness,
since connections,
since we lit up the day.

Now above us the sky
where cloud shadows swim
reflected in your grey eyes once blue.
I never thought you'd be a grandmother,
feeding swans by summer lakes,
fixing bike seats with screwdrivers,
buying ice-cream,
painting cartoons,
pointing out bats once again
very déjà vu.

I Miss You

You used to bang doors at fourteen.
Fell asleep once, a train driver from Abercynon plucked you
from sweet dreams of sun-kissed desert islands
and dusky, sugared babes
on the bench beneath the old clock.

They thought you broke that world record, shovelling coal,
on the *Mallard* or something similarly fowl,
you were dirty-faced like a fresh-aired collier,
the wind in your hair and soot in your lungs.

Then to Catterick to run in big, black boots,
you could shoot a gnat's bollocks off at fifty yards,
got a badge on your shoulder for it, always won the teddy,
carnie's hated you, fuck the goldfish,
'I want that bunny
for her', my mam.

You learnt how to connect circuits in the Middle East,
whilst fighting the Muslim Brotherhood,
dived for giant clams in the Canal
and made them into lampshades to sell to the ragheads.
Saw Tripoli, El Alamein and ate bacon in Alexandria,
flew over the Pyramids,
marched through sand
for a Queen you never voted for.

Brought a skill home, became a communist in Swindon.
I was so proud of you, practicing what you preached,
never breaking a promise, like the time you gave me ten pence
when I punched Cleary's face in after the bastard bit a hole in my back.

I was only six years old,
me with my Roman shield, him all Saxon and wild as that storm,
when you carried me from the car, across the flooded road,
made me safe as houses. Always.

From the cratered cycle track, overgrown with dandelions
you can just about make out the crumbling factory walls.
The place where oil stuck to overalls as pink blossom would gum
to brides
and tumours snuck up on you when the radio was loud,
when the tea stained that old work bench and the young boys
marvelled at you solving the executioner's jigsaw puzzles
with rainbow cables the size of their legs.

One time, me and Pies cleaned for two weeks,
metal green machines, a hand-high layer of dust.
Then someone showed us the tarantulas,
squashed cobalt blue, they'd stowed away
between silk sheets all the way from Mandalay.
There was a python from India once,
and old Ken's locker full of stolen tools,
page three girls sellotaped across my teenage eyes,
cotton from Pakistan,
skip quality control after Friday beers,
and the alcoholic engineer in his white shirt
covered in grease and dirt
and the warnings about steam stripping skin,
the men telling us about the Scottish trip
and the loose women on Princes Street.

We'd watch the news,
argue about rights and wrongs and fair play.
Scream at the rugby, have hope for the future,
live dreams in living rooms.

I'd shuffle your videos of Dad's Army and Last of the Summer
Wine,
talk about university, watch you play FAT down the club,
and smile at your holiday brochures.

I don't go there much now
but the other day I rode past,
where strip-lights used to shine brightly in that dead place,
just midnight cowboys enter now
and camera freaks with Photoshop stares,
an urban decay paradise, like old hospitals,
flaking paint, woodworm doors
and rats in shadows,
scurrying from a forgotten great past.

What happened to all those faces?
What happened to all those words?
Where did those moments go?
Why did you have to go?
Against your will I know,
I miss you.

Isolation

She is my friend,
my comfort blanket.
My favourite chair,
the moment when the sun breaks through the clouds.
The smile across the table,
the pat upon the back.
The kiss upon the neck,
at our secret picnic spot.
Cwtch you.
The bend beneath the castle
and the initials carved in that teenage tree.

Cardiff

The coal merchant of the world,
bottleneck of Jew, Norwegian, Somali, Yemini, Caribbean, Italian,
  Spanish, Irish and Greek,
the Congo of canals,
of commerce and commuters
where the richest man in the world
moved iron and steel,
was a digger of docks,
the zoot-zone Zeitgeist,
amniotic albumen,
Google Map placenta,
he sucked in more Saxons and Normans
like flies round a wound,
like ants to the sugar
but some wondered at wonders unfolding
and remembered what happened
after the Romans deserted
when they hung aboriginal traitors
in cold castles and called
us foreign in our own land.

Waking still-drunk on whisky within these foreign walls
I can feel the cool grey birth of salt-kissed calls
of the gulls as they gouge out my gristle breath
and you touch me with tender-tip fingers
beneath the sheets near the old *Bucket of Blood*,
still dream-like, devouring coarse jazz,
muggle French food in the *Snakepit*,
my past-pulse pitted
as out on the pavement
steam rises from people like ghosts.

With lungs once louder than Liverpool and London
you built markets and merchants and mosques,
welcomed sailors and thieves and James Bond singers.
The docks were a cauldron of hip,
coloured with charisma, we were tonality corner,
a mash up of wooden whales,
iron horses and their shunters -
builders and brokers,
packet steamers and painted ladies.

But now the sea birds are singing,
serenading your lips fresh as mango
that came all the way from Cuba.
I see the fog out the trough of the window,
rising over the sea-swell soft cough
that's lapping a pink sunlit dawn
and we are sweetness in the city of sin.

As I rise from my slumber,
pull on my jeans like rivets,
you become a memory
of sun-skulled African shores,
a *Tiger* in my pocket
to keep as a trinket
as eel-thin workers shovel smoke
in the League of Nations.

Turkish Chip Shop

Mehmet sang when he spoke
and his eyes flamed when he saw us,
he was a shadow puppet with a menu for a scrim.
Working seven days a week up on Whitchurch Road,
he would dance, shake and laugh all at once.
And it must have seemed to him like it was every night
that I dodged the anxious falling rain,
too tired to cook, the old man will save us,
him pleased with himself and our culture
because with every fried potato he sold
a brick would be laid next to another,
to be battered by the holy sun
on a picturesque hilltop far away from this land,
this land no longer watched over by God.

Poured People

if not out of the clickety-clack,
as the cold wind carries over the water
there's always the motorway bubble tube for all,
those private tombs, where insanity rules,
washed and waxed and waned on weekends.
Made mine with music, my left-hand choice,
just a brief moment of me, free of flowers,
free of child locks, free of conversation
that might ricochet off the walls, the air-con dealing
with the scent of sandalwood, lead and chromium,
red as lips, faded SPF and stale baby milk…

And then it's auto-pilot into the concrete box
with the Grand Prix corners and sardined zones.
Then out into the day, all important, yes you'd say,
much more important, than you, or it, or me.
I see a mirror and lose it momentarily
as I thread between skyscrapers,
dodge plastic bottles held like swords,
coffee cups with lids that keep my secret safe,
sidestep the gypsy, the mafia gangs
'No thanks, I don't want a Big Issue,
I'll give my beans to the ex-soldier in the sleeping bag.'

Leather on carpets, a glide and a glance
over parapets of terraced computer monitors,
there are windows in this exhibit
for the seagulls pleasure.
And later next to desks, or skulking behind plants,
camouflaged in white stains,
there is time again to mate, to recreate the perfect lie.
The harmony of ritualization, like a bird call,

a sound wave or a frequency,
eyes that say 'go out with me, fancy me, pity me'
but never rely on me, in such a fantasy game.

But soon the ratio of lusts is swapping graphs,
as each second passes we get closer to you
and less connected to you.
You with your red shoes and your yellow brick road
to the wasted and unwanted,
tick-tock, pay scale clock
of diminishing returns on the least investment
while no-one notices the crows on the windowsill.
Only when you leave do you become whole again,
if only briefly, crave wine or ale, take the bus home
to delay the cycle of DNA decay.

Gentrification

Where once there were drunken Irishmen
fighting with fists and bottles
now there are bearded lumberjacks with ponytails
heading to coffee bars on oversized girls bikes.
Discussing their next project, afraid of the forest,
sipping latte from Honduras, in slipper-soft shoes,
buying craft ale, locally, on their MacBook.
I stroll those ancient streets searching for memories
of the old Polish Spitfire pilot, the West Indian houngan,
the Catholic clairvoyant and the red-light lady with large bust
but no one in the bespoke talking buildings
remembers these corpses long gone.
They're more interested in the new scramble for Europe,
black the new white, the future is red,
vintage the new décor, selective in their causes,
yet confused by the Balfour declaration.
Happy to be raped by an ape, *blah blah*,
but still they call the privileged pot pink.
Pop, point, pout, meme me,
then give in to the bankers,
dredging their digits through the city's faded rubble,
they're fingering Lego bricks in a toy box,
searching for that right piece, come hither
to solve all our puzzles.

For David Neville

Dreaming of the coloured noise
and those oak-leaved green hills,
carpeted in the summertime
with hemlock and daisies.
Running through the ferns,
sipping cider on the rocks,
watching girls much older
tumbling in long grass
by the bright August moon.
We followed footprints in the dirt,
spied on steamed-up cars
down the darkest, farm track lanes.
Oh I can still remember,
we had such carefree ways,
when every day was Valentine's Day,
nothing gained, nothing lost,
when nothing was always a lot.
But almost fifty years later
when it would probably be better
if certain memories were killed,
I can still see your white-blonde hair,
the Christmas jumper, all red and cream.
I suppose we've all just forgotten,
I mean, who could comprehend a shotgun?
And your baby sister too, just an innocent angel.
We still went to school, just carried on
like nothing had happened.
Played in those same fields
where you would have grown up
to gallop great horses
through fields blanketed with sheep.
Nowadays we meet occasionally,

talk of village talk,
laugh at the long-dead flashers and paedophiles,
smirk about the bullied ones,
rub a chin that's scarred and bruised,
mention kids today,
feel pity for the old folk
who died under Welsh earth or in French mud
with respect in our voices.
We yak of our own dead ones,
a brief second of remembrance
all they get,
for we are here now, still here,
in our time of dying.
And though some of us
have been around the world
and back, even we just carry on.
What else is there to do?

Christmas Dad

There's flowers by the hanging tree on a frosty New Years Day.
Mist circles the clock tower, I wonder how long it'll stay?

I'm underwater, thinking about my own daughter.
I'm all adrift, floundering like a shipwrecked freighter.

Floating like a lead weight, only just submerged.
All my heartaches on the motorway, breath converged.

Scratching the surface, clawing, fingers through air.
Empty stomach, filling in a mental health questionnaire.

Lacking love, like Plath's oven door.
Tired of trying to keep score.

Sleepy now I head home heavy.
But I'll return later like a bad penny.

And sure enough, after a day of rest.
When newspapers still know best.

I watch the sky stain with fire.
As other parents call you vampire.

'Fancy doing that to your little kids, on Christmas too.'
But I think I understand how difficult it is to colour blue.

We're driving up the Skeleton Coast

a cold north wind is blowing.
We stop to take photos of the *Zelia India*,
the sand soaked by sea mist.
I try to speak but the waves loose thunder
and your foamy breath rains down persistent needles of ice
as we challenge the Benguela and her bleached manes of sea
through fog in this graveyard so free.
We carry on, stop off at a favourite surf spot,
listen to the wind soaring through dunes
and think of the thousand crushed vessels,
henna-like under a silver sun, rusting like burnt cars,
russet roped, chestnut chains cankered
at 'The Gates of Hell'.
And no more towns now, for three hundred miles,
not until we reach Angola.

We stop at Cape Cross to see the seals.
In easy fractions of a million, we spy a single pup,
early as they come, born into a changing climate.
Last week you told us how you stood across the iron bell rock,
yards from a hyena, a stand down ensued,
you offered the odd beer, cold as the vast sky.

Later you talked to the car wash boys
as we cruised the shanty town, past pink hotels,
blue barbers and green bars with *Beemers* and *Mercs* -
the ironic spoils of a distant racist war.
I remember we cried in Windhoek at the museum display
but I hope we meet again, my Californian friend,
in a warm pub in Cardiff
and we can tell more tales of spears and tanks
and horses and deserts.

When an 18hr train ride became 23

I kissed you after we left Soweto,
felt your hot breath in Mafeking,
ran to see Baden Powell,
danced under that revolver,
waved by that drug-crazed policeman,
eyes wide back in sanctuary,
laughing at the passport stamps.
Then we ate some oranges,
got nuts through the open window.
The anticipation was unbearable
as we postponed for the border.
Our carnal signal, listening to the whistle of the tracks.
It didn't take us long after the guard checked our ticket
to lock the door and peer out on the desert,
at Botswana ambling by,
at the yellow sun,
that was owned by us and nobody else,
not even a thousand gods.
I remember you sitting on me,
I remember you squinting at the stars,
I remember you merging with the moon,
far across those savage sands.

We had enough beer for a week
and a handful of food,
so it wasn't a problem
when we stopped for five hours,
to gaze upon the overturned wagons,
the cargo of corn spilled on the tracks.
I took a photograph.
I still have it somewhere,
35mm, economic,

we made love again,
to replenish the memories,
use what might one day be lost.
You drank another Castle,
I slept in your breast.

And the weird thing about Bulawayo,
a dawn we weren't attached to,
was that the adventure was only just beginning,
in that place of slaughter
we met kindness and revolution in equal measure.
I bought a Thomas Maputo cassette
in the local supermarket,
sat by the pool,
grazed on warthog and tomatoes,
talked politics with a smile not a frown,
melted into that perfect night
and never once dreamt of growing old with you,
but yet here I am.

Etosha to Okavango

The red sun is dark over the great white place,
as rhino and tembo play truth or dare.
Across the yellow water while plovers referee
the sighs and camera clicks mean that someone's there.

Soundtrack surreal, we sit on a wooden bench,
inhale the dust, *feed the head.*
Hear hyenas laugh deep into the night
at your amorous liaison, 'neath that sun so red.

Near the mopane plains that stretch for countries
we cross the border, heading towards Ghanzi.
Throw away tomatoes, pass a million purple trees
in a flat land, brushed bush, rolling carefree.

Until a new world wakes in a new wet dawn,
the water an oasis, you can literally breathe it in.
Camping on an island hear the lion roar
distant as dreams that we're already within.

Over the Cwm

For Lili

I watch your eyes as Earth's shadow falls upon you
and you become my sun, all hazel with flecks of gold and black.
I watch you lift a petal heavy with dew.
Your nose became nature's scaffold.
And I swear I saw a smile escape, subtle as a burglar.

Ivy silhouette, the giant trees by the river,
not a shadow stirred, then the blood moon.
How did we ever get so lost?
A day spellbound in an ancient place.
I'm not sure how to take the you out of me.

Sunset over Penally

Far from this window on a July day,
I watch the last fragments fade away.
Red sun falling into the empty sea,
today has gone, far away from me.

And the midnight sand that is glowing blue
is not worth arguing about with you.
The oystercatchers call like a squeaky door,
my dog has one last run upon the shore.

How still the water this peaceful night,
as old men sleep in cottages out of sight.
I watch the stars on the leaden surface,
tomorrow I'll pack my final suitcase.

Haiku

squeezing into their seats
two women talk about diets
- KFC

mountain and clouds
becoming one
- after sunset

it's just me
and the moon now
- empty bus stop

tired eyes follow
the migrating geese
- slow train

less cockle pickers
every year
- tide turning

Tết

'In war no one wins or loses, there is only destruction.'
- Bao Ninh (North Vietnamese Army Veteran)

The torn and tattered black pyjamas,
dog-eared and infused with blood,
tell of the new moon in '68
when we crept silently towards Huế,
south of the Perfume River.
I can still taste the bamboo soup
bubbling on the breeze,
and the copper sweat of fire
battling fiercely with apricot blossom.
But when it got really tough I thought of you -
expelled from school, exiled for thirty years.
You were a cook's helper on a French liner,
sailed to New York, shovelled snow in London,
took photos in Paris, read Lenin.
Stole rice from the Japanese
just to feed your people,
fought for peace, wrote poetry
from inside a Chinese jail
and now, sick with TB, as an old man
I knew you were watching over me.
And when spring finally came,
threading through smoke and tears,
we walked home, left our brothers behind
and remembered what it was like
to watch dragon dancers in the street
and origami fish hanging
on the tiny hands of children.

Somewhere near Barcelona

you said I tasted of sugar-sweet mustard
in broken English and speedball Spanish.

I saw you first in that dripping jazz bar,
if you don't count the Internet, of course.
It was there that I asked for your autograph,
with your eyes as brown as leather
and your pretty blue dress like the weather.

We chatted for more than an hour,
ate *Pulpo a feira*, drank a fruity red.
I laughed when you told me about pineapple.
Fell in love quickly, like a child entering the playground,
made it last longer than your movies.
We were beautiful as swans on winter lakes,
crocheted fingers, arched half moon,
smothered you in cock and kisses.

Watched you snoring like a puppy,
brushed your long blonde hair,
from your cadaverous face.
Premiered your dreams,
saw a tear escape
and thought maybe you'd tried too hard,
to be that perfect baby your father had to have.

Out of the Depth

'The first morning we had sharks.'
It was a week before they dropped Little Boy.
We soon forgot all about our own big bang though,
the fire's glow that lit up the tropical night
with groaning metal, twisted alloy,
the coating of boiling oil,
the fissured bones
and the dribbling of blood
into the briny ocean…

drip,
drip,
drip…

I was one part in nine hundred,
a long way from landlocked Kentucky,
not good odds – we prayed to Saint Nicholas
and kept watch for lost albatross
to keep Davy Jones at bay.

drip,
drip,
drip…

Our circle of white feet danced beneath a red dawn,
while whistling *fuka* touch our collars –
a new special splashed on the *carte de jour.*

In four days the cruel sun took our skin
while the salt terrorised minds
with the *duppy* of Jonah.

'Water, water, everywhere, nor any drop to drink.'
Through swollen tongues we spoke. Split lips to smile.
I ate rotten potatoes off a pelagic table,
part of the bobbing banquet
as we waited patiently to be plucked
out of the screaming surf.

Note: Corporal Edgar Harrell was a Marine, just 20-years-old, who survived the Japanese torpedoing of the USS Indianapolis in 1945. Of the 1196 crew only 316 survived, many were killed by sharks. He tells his remarkable story in his book 'Out of the Depth'.

Belle de Jour

At first, she is afraid of the blind puppeteer,
of being tied up and teased,
has flashbacks to that holy man
who took everything from #MeToo
Says to her betrothed, *'sovegna vos a temps de ma dolor'*.

Oh Séverine my pearl, you must wake up, here are some roses!
I watch you with your embroidery
and feel the power in that hollow.
I see your sucked in chalice,
that pink mouth, such a waste in the afternoon sun.

So she becomes the new lupa:
a secret sheathed vice
for the gangsters and gentlemen.
'Let us go and make our visit' they say.
What is the meaning of it all?

OK, come to me you poor man.
Let me make your gender lewd again.
Get down on your knees, enjoy your pantomime
but don't shoot the messenger
I am only for sharing.

Trivial things

It's funny how you remember the little things,
inconsequential things, like you twirling around my cell
in that over-sized red jumper, so much love
you had poured into that wool.

That time when it was absolute, frenzied after the baby news
when we became as one just like the poets.

I remember when you snatched that plant, a withered bloom, it
didn't matter what, you bee-lined towards my desk and without so
much as a wink to the scientific journals you took it upon yourself
to be my saviour, my seamless angel, my teacher of everything that
truly mattered and became all those other gods rolled into one.

But now in the harsh light of downhill futures,
the ruins of cinemas, the rubble of bedsits, the draining of the lake,
the crumbling of the pavements and rotting of those autumn leaves
that were the gold we kicked to the sky and the rain, or the
abandoned piles of stones from mountain farms…
all I want to do is crawl back inside of you, to catch one last
moment, a pure minute of all that was once so picture-perfect.

Dancer

You mentioned sex,
casually,
like we'd recently experienced a long spell of sunshine.
Carefully selecting adjectives for the old days
like you were picking fruit,
said we were amazing at least once.
Earlier in the evening you'd told me you weren't happy.
I said I was sorry to hear that.
We walked the same familiar streets like time had stood still,
oblivious of thirty years of hesitation.
I'd know your shape anywhere
and you hadn't forgotten my hands, apparently.
Then a taxi appeared out of the blue
with so much talking still to do.
Don't know about you
but I swear the city lights dimmed
just a little bit when you went back to him.

Porphyra

You are beautiful yet few of us really see you.
Spend half your life in hiding
the other half being baked in the sun,
your pink fronds full of calcium are used to scour worms,
your peacock's tail fans the years away
and we can taste your acidic truffle
you iodine cloud maker
living for a hundred years.

Relax on the beach, intertidal, like deckchairs and picnics,
drape your spaghetti hair over those prehistoric rocks,
compare notes on The Battle of Britain and last week's migrant
  invasion
while in that trendy bar uptown
your Celtic crisp is dusted on sea bass.
Yet only the Japanese immortalise Drew-Baker,
as the mother of the sea,
at the Sumiyoshi shrine.

Bebe the Pomeranian made it to Lifeboat 7

The thing about ice you see,
the thing about ice…
is that it doesn't really smell of anything.
Not like that filet mignon you fed me so tenderly -
my miniature lion's head cushioned in your gloved hand,
oh, and that poached salmon, the chicken Lyonnaise and foie gras,
well, what's a dog to do?

A large Arctic air mass allowed the stars to come out to play
and when the temperature dropped the sea became glass.

It was a night to remember alright. Sun Yat Sen was licking Punch Romaine from the hand of Mr Harper (of Harper & Row publishers),
Mrs Elizabeth Rothschild's mutt was admiring the Palace of Versailles,
while I finished off the roast pigeon and lamb with a mint sauce that was simply to die for.

At 11:40pm Murdoch's call came too late though,
the diamond floe cut us to the bone
and soon the ocean came in, unprejudiced.

I thought about the orange-flavoured ice, drenched in champagne.
Oh yes, I just lapped it up…
then I heard shouting, I smelt the briny swell, the ripples and rush,
the scent of fear on children's lips, foam and roll,
my fleas gripping tight as babies cried…

I cocked my head sideways,
I hear *my* Master's Voice above the crush of the sea
and the band played '*Nearer, My God, to Thee*'.

When we reached New York I saw the dark shadow of a gull
which made the sign of the cross on the water.
Fifteen hundred someone barked.
And now?
Well, alas, I can still hear poor Frou-Frou,
screaming for mercy,
teeth tearing at Helen's dress.

Note: Of all the animals aboard the RMS Titanic during her disastrous maiden voyage, in 1912, only three dogs survived.

Far from Plain Jayne

I know that you're working from home this week
'cos you tell me every time we meet.
And it's funny how we constantly linger
over summer fields hot with lust.
You with your Greek island tan,
the Ray Bans, the loose cotton dress.
If I didn't know better I'd suspect you,
like a detective with kinky murder on his mind.
But no, what the hell am I thinking?
You with your brandy-brown eyes
and your russet hair,
those succulent lips,
your childbearing hips
and those breasts that were sculptured by gods.
You talk of our mothers
and earthly pursuits
like gardening and walking and yet
there's something I can't quite imagine
though many misty mornings I've tried.
Perhaps I should just stick you in maybe
the box that's overflowing with your kind.

Outlaw

A WANTED poster in the window of the Spanish restaurant
he visibly shrinks at the mug shot staring back
but quickly slinks into body traffic,
is cloaked by bus emissions,
anointed by drizzle pausing at the café door.
Heads for the table at the back,
grabs a copy of The Times,
scans the MI5 lonely hearts
as a coffee cup bounces near his bare feet.
He recalls playing Russian roulette with umbrellas
on the Piccadilly Line,
those days spent sweating, listening
to Rwandan radio…
moated by tourists now
as the rain turns to snow outside.
Sneaking glances he sees them everywhere:
the baby with the miniature microphone,
the round-eyed Korean and his Nikon lens,
the old lady's cyanide hatpin,
the Arab and the Uzi,
even the waitress cutting cake
and the sad dog tied up to the lamppost with string.
The next voice you hear,
the next voice you hear
will be your own.
And then suddenly he notices the other passengers,
vacant faces left on the shelves
like last season's ski boots,
mindful of getting snagged on coat hooks,
sipping pink tea with pumpkin pie,
flaying yesterdays in small rooms,
licking the soft spoons,

turning pages of magazines, biding time.
He'll welcome the flamingo-coloured morning
and then escape once more
to join the alphabet of the uncaring city
where he'll star in his own silent movies.

European Tinder

Once upon a riverbank a church was built upon the mud next to the snaking Seine. And over the centuries more stinking, starving peasants were given bread to submit to the will of richer men. Then those gothic architects, who'd neglected to teach the parishioners to read carved chimera and gargoyles in the poor people's book that Notre Dame became, added a few Strix, who would eat human flesh, just in case anyone got ideas of revolution. Then for eight hundred years or more it stood as a symbol of all that was chic until holy Easter week, when buttresses glowed, rib vaults cracked and rose windows roasted. And as modern Parisians, who worship at cafes, were sparked into song they could only watch as smoke seeped out, the cathedral ceiling a fresco of stars. Children filmed it all on iPhones and the media told us what to believe, a little like priests and liars. We now have collective grief for the oak roof finally freed to flames, for the stones not the mountains, for the wood not the trees. Then just as quickly as the inferno went out we heard that hundreds of millions were pouring in, a pyre of piety, scorched to the soul. We will rebuild it said the rich men to the world, then someone alluded to a French 9/11, but don't panic, for order was quickly restored as we got sucked back to the diverse crowd on TV. But don't you see the problem? Seems we're swiping the wrong way. And as newspapers and camera crews re-educate and wash the mind no one notices a small tallow-turning tapeworm, adjusting her headscarf, before scurrying off, like a sewer rat to the Chapelle-Pajol district with a black crow shadowing her in the form of a smiling bearded chaperone.

Blood River

Instagram will not immortalise the soft passage of my palm across the taut curves of your stomach or darkest thighs as I pause briefly to let the tropical temperature rise and a breath to be caught, brusquely, while the red dusk sky invokes the perfume of your breath to silence the spirits of the forest. And not even those smatterings of hot fingertips tracing contours around my spine as our tongues become entangled, like great raptors upon the wind, can be digitised on a hard disk far from here as the feathers fall and fester but that brief moment for me, will pulse forever Congo.

Wet morning

a woodpecker with crimson cap and Zorro eyes
hops from one termite mound to the next
as the rain bounces off the grass
and gauges itself on gigantic oak leaves
before tipping like a bucket outside a temple

Sarah

Back in '85 I asked to borrow a pencil from you.
You looked surprised but still smiled.
Sat on your own at the back of the hall,
a force field of impending rejection surrounding you.
We didn't stand a chance, none of us, no way.
Just realised I forgot to say how much I loved you.
Not that I didn't have the chance.
I had several in fact.
Down by the river at midnight,
watching our stars sprinkle themselves on the water.
But other people got in the way,
that's my excuse anyway.
And I loved plenty of course,
sometimes too much.
While you waited in the wings of my theatre of destruction,
always there, always on hand, always...
I remember you just picked up a guitar one day
and wrote songs in a notebook that were better than mine.
Whatever happened to that muse?
That straight and true, that diamond blue, that oozing clue
that melted my heart every time I looked at you.
And now we are in different time zones,
I'm terraced in while you're free near leafy farms.
Tell me some things I've forgot...
about how I was always nice to you.
Like that time you left your drunken bike
at the foot of my creaking stairs.
When you offered yourself to my warm embrace
but instead of parading you truth I lay guard next to you
like a faithful dog and with silent kisses protected you
from the cold and dangerous night
that I'd become, until you were well enough,

well enough to run away from me forever.
Yes. Of course I do.
Now, I wish I'd been bad.
Wish I'd done all the things they said I already had.
But don't you see?
I couldn't do right for doing wrong
and often think about
all they took away from me,
and maybe all they took away from us.

Angelystor

It must have been about the time
that the Sumerians started first grade
and began scribbling Photoshop Custom Shapes on clay.
A careless hawfinch just left me for dead,
that's all I can remember anyway.
Sometimes I forget those childish things
but what I did learn from those chatty waxwings,
as the summers purred passed, was that brave Welsh warriors
are buried at Stonehenge. And yes I've been scared before.
Like when I felt bears scratching at my metatarsal roots and I saw
the deadly flames from the bronze axe foundry.
Not long after that Jesus died and my mother bled red
in Llangernyw. And then, in about five hundred years or so,
hardy men put slate upon stone upon stone
and listened for the honey-howling wind
that told of death through mead dreams
as the goblins and ghouls flew all around.
I remember like yesterday Hywel Dda riding past
and I whinnied through the storm to his horse for a bit.
Then a tall man came and snapped a young arm
and made a bow to kill a squirrel.
Nowadays though I just get men in white coats
who come to caress and mutilate my gnarled skin.
I overhear them - talking of curing cancer.
Most days though I just sit, peaceful like,
dreaming of when they'll leave this green world forever.
I hear from the vagabond beetles that it won't be long.
Not if they keep burning my friends in Brazil anyway.

Spaceman

I see the best minds of my generation wiped clean by corporate banality, battered by camouflaged-screaming righteous beatniks, cultureless anti-punks, who barricade our smiles and use zeros and ones to cut out our tongues, while censoring the asphyxiated air waves, they smother and clog, put you in a brainwash bubble, alone with your Paxil pills, suicide chills, put on a treadmill with two extreme choices – choose wisely or it's the dentist's drill, a lunatic bladed windmill, round and round, dizzy yet? And then when you're proper drowning, killed in a gill net or tied to the sawmill rack they'll drape a bombed-flag veil, encrypt synapses once again and suffocate the digital planet with a tricolour of shame, shut out authenticity, block ruthlessly until the scenery of your screens, the place you used to call free, is frozen by snowflakes that thread gently, without warning, sneaking into your oxygen tanks to diffuse ice into your black and brown blood until the silence is complete.

The sky like the morning after ashes
just me and the dog
quiet as stones
naked apart from my shorts
day dreaming by the stream
watching a wren
skip across the fallen oaks…

If I saw you today would you still have that flower in your hair?
The one that used to nestle in that forest of enchantment,
pink on brunette, matching your lips of Rose wine,
the Joan Collins smile, the shyness of your mind,
and all those carefully considered dreams and horoscopes,
like a yellow brick road that led towards the temple –
our enlightenment lost on our youth.
Now. In a peripheral hallucination I stare at the fridge,

where every year, a new magnet, reminds us of a far away foreign land, a tick off the list, perhaps a city break or slow stroll around a book fair with your castrated Major Tom.

Perhaps 50 : Fifty was too generous
and that's why there seems more behind than in front.
Like when the sun shone on a Roath Park morning in a city where all love was mine. Where I watched you skip along the water's edge and all my dreams they came alive.
Your ice cream melting like a Monet in the museum before closing time, skating through those golden leaves with your chestnut eyes dangerous as an autumn obsolescence when
I didn't want to miss a single second.

Now we have apps for this and that,
wildcats sat on prayer mats, chitchat with vampire bats, mud flats and thermostats, crooked hats during coup d'états…

Perhaps they want it this way,
but seriously, I don't think they think at all.
They're just spacemen in helmets floating in darkness,
blind to the fragile, killing nature of all that surrounds them,
dead to the love and oblivious to birdsong,
imprisoned by the fences they stake,
ignorant of impending earthquakes,
they cultivate heartaches with no hand brake
while trying to knock down walls that
only exist in their septic minds.

Hunchback

I'm sitting in the car, waiting for my mam who is in the doctors.
I see him walking towards me like a one-legged man,
deliberately, with purpose, defining slow.
The hunchback wears a long, blue smock.
He might have been Van Gogh in a previous life.
He has one stick (standard hospital issue) and one umbrella
(standard charity shop).
His head is down - he is a connoisseur of pavements,
has an appreciation of gum, vomit and the secret life of ants.
He bends to pick some litter, a flyer from a local rock band,
he pockets it for later, for what reason I don't know.
Maybe to help him light a fire?
Carries on his journey that transforms to endurance.
Passes my jeep with the open window,
ignores the sweet sound of an old Chuck Prophet CD
as my arm catches the spring sun,
the sun he never sees.
I feel sad for no reason,
perhaps I see me, perhaps I see all of us.
I wonder if he used to be a farmer
or if he used to abuse children.
Did he used to work in a bank, beat his ugly wife?
Was he a speechwriter for a Prime Minister?
Like that dull old bat who feeds rats and swears at the moon.
Was he a famous poet or a factory hand?
Maybe a great footballer or a thief?
Then my mother returns from her visit
and snaps me out of my trance.
'All OK?'
'Yeh, lets go home,' she says.

Flame retardant

Tell me you don't love me one more time
I need to hear it straight from your sweet lips.
After I've shown you the best years of my lives
I still feel the need to hold rejection close.

But instead of just leaving you behind
and flying to the stars on my own clear path
I loiter by the toilet block you created
and pray I'll start a fire that will consume.

I'll stand so close I'll feel the heat upon me
I'll cheer as the inferno jumps across.
Watch as your many worlds go up in smoke
laugh as your veneer is peeled away.

At the end of the day I know I'm right
for every time you raise your bloody sword
you make me stronger in the audience's eyes
and I'll still be standing when they see you fall.

The cup of the world

last night I stopped the car and looked down on the old city that is so lost to us now in a haze of sea mist and memory and just for a moment I was dragged back to a time when colour lived in us all like clouds that became circus trapeze artists flying through dreams like spirits dancing reflected in the mirror of supermarket glass while magic carpets took us high above the volcano erupting as the rubberneckers absorb the crash scene on the M4 past Aberavon a time when we filled the cup of the world with hope over cider and whisky and remembered that smoky club smooching in the shadows you etched a flower in my heart taught me to read and showed me how to look at masterpieces in the museum his washed up colours flowing over you like rain in that fresh autumn night before the rugby against Fiji before the walk to paradise when you grabbed my hand after bolting wine and swaying in time to Otis Redding and that guy who thought you were a movie star and later huddling into each other as we walked past the Italian where you used to serve tables burning our youth into the night and each other and wishing those minutes would be our everlasting legacy

Cabinda

Look! The Bakongo are here – beautiful and strong
honey-sweet fat caterpillar-lipped
tasting of frangipani in dew,

statuesque curves adorned in psychedelic charms…
Open that casket, give the men nzimbu shells
and tell them to wash off that sugar sweat of jungle.

Then check the chains are tight,
they'll shrink down to the bones
by the time we reach port at Charleston.

I can see that one now, put in virginal white,
that cassava belly starved away,
in a silk gown and a flower in her hair.

And the other one, there, yes the one with all her teeth.
She'll be worth a thousand dollars one day,
depending on those hips of course.

Now don't forget the trinkets for our good friends,
measure out the copper, the cloth and the beads
and double-check the figures in the ledger.

Good Day

It was a great day to find out I was dead.
I suppose half of me was expecting it,
the other half was too ill to care.
I remember looking out the window,
starting to feel a little stronger.
The cherry blossom on the trees was so beautiful,
there was a soft breeze
and pretty nurses smiled
before it all changed, forever,
such a small word
that can make a million memories
come flooding back so quickly
yet they don't make a dent,
don't scratch the surface,
are less than a tear in the ocean
and it was then that I learnt
that some things are best left unknown,
better to live in blissful ignorance
like an old dog who faithfully follows
into the small room
where walls press upon your chest
but for me it must be different
there has to be another way out,
an unopened door,
a fresh treatment,
a new hope.
Tonight I will eat meat and vegetables
and not taste a thing,
I suppose the pain will go too
when the disc is wiped,
the files deleted.
OK no time to lose,

a taxi home,
hard heart and acceptable crying,
lots of yes, lots of no,
spring clean, kick-start,
organise my life support,
get ready for the final safari,
look my loved ones
dead in the eye,
get angry with someone I don't believe in,
curse and swear
as light creeps on in
through half closed curtains
and I see so clearly now
like an eagle in her prime
but then all too soon
I'm making lists
of things to do and see
while I throw away possessions
and collect each sun followed by a moon
as precious minutes scroll by
I'm already planning what to say
when all my love goes out
in my mind's eye
when I'm bone dry
or I drip-dry
beneath that blue sky.

Laika

Although it was cold, so very cold, on the streets of Moscow at least we had each other. Huddled in doorways, scurrying through subways, riding the train to Red Square, scavenging beneath St Basils, wandering through Gorky and begging for frankfurters or boiled sausage outside the backdoors of restaurants and lapping up *kefir* from the drains. As a baby I'd been brave, learning to survive on the streets like that but when they took me and confined me in that small cage I have to admit I was a little bit scared. Then came the laxatives and the centrifuges and the scalpel cuts bathed with iodine. Dr Yazdovsky let me play with his children a while and for those brief minutes I had high hopes for the future. I was quiet and charming so they say. But when you gave me that final kiss on the nose I suppose deep down inside I knew my destiny lay among the stars. Alone, in silence, I watched the world spinning round, one thousand miles below. Then on the fourth lap I felt the temperature rise and I suppose I just shut my eyes for a moment. I was only three years old.

Alois

Out of the blue
Eve hands me the phone.
'Say hello to Alois.'
Suddenly I'm catapulted back through time
across the continent, over seas, deserts, lakes.
Your voice as warm as African sand,
the delay on the line a campfire yarn,
the memory of your big black frame
and the vision of you fighting a lion.
I want to shake your shovel of a hand
and sit in silence to watch tuskers drink at dusk,
neither of us speaking to understand.
You say you're not too far from Cape Town now.
I mention meeting up in Vic Falls,
to ride through Zambia and Malawi,
you say it would be a pleasure.
And I have thoughts of old Nairobi town,
the streets you'd own and I your shadow.
In life there are certain men you meet
who will carve a mark upon your soul.
We are lucky and privileged to know
a tiny morsel of you, big Al.

Goshawk

If you might thread your way
through the pine forest up above
the ancient oak and holly trees
having crossed the clear, cold stream
past the hazelnut and blackberry rows
once you leave the old path behind
you will feel the soft damp carpet
of brown needles beneath your feet
and be walled by silent echoes
only broken by the screams
of dark corvids bawling in peril
or squirrels scampering fast
as the goose hawk unfurls a claw
and the paradise is shattered
as a handsome murderer hops
along a fallen conifer branch
before sensing your giant shadow
and disappearing all too soon.

Blade

The cold concrete is your warm bed now
while the artificial snow smells of flowers.
Irrigating eyes blur the mustard moon
and your blood is finger-licking good.
You have no thoughts of stone boats – it's too soon,
'cos you have double Geography on Monday morning
and you want to learn much more about Jamaica.
But as a siren wails somewhere in this circus town
and your fist unfurls like a fern in monochrome
perhaps that boy with the bigger blade
will think of you on his short drive home.

Pure Heart

he sits
next to the tatty armchair
still as a china dog
on the mantelpiece

then gets up
wanders about the house
like a teenager
on Valentines Day

sighs a big sigh
then settles down
into the well-worn carpet
like it's summer grass

hears the ticking of the clock
but still can't count
as the sun sets again
he'll sleep a little

hasn't eaten much for weeks
scared to take too long
in the frosty garden
just in case you come back

maybe today?
then more sighs
and eyes as big as the moon
the occasional whine

alone in a sad world
his stamina his torture
faithfulness
a prison

you wish you could reach him
set him free
you try to give love
but he pulls away

he wants to be happy
but only one thing will do
and that's him
not you

but it's too late now
and soon the dust
will multiply
and peace will come

Haiku

meadow art
red clover, eyebright and forget-me-nots
summer outfits in the beer garden

for the 'leavers'
the biggest turnout yet
- EU elections

the decisive vote in
National Grid surges
with chitter-chatter

the visitor's book
still unsigned
- hospice reception

two names in a heart
washed from the sand
- winter waves

‘I’m just sittin' here watchin' the wheels go round and round
I really love to watch them roll
No longer ridin' on the merry-go-round
I just had to let it go’
- John Lennon / Yoko Ono

Notes

The following author notes are to help explain certain references in some of the poems. They are in no way complete and I certainly do not wish to discourage further interpretation or dissection of the poems but simply to point the more serious researcher towards more relevant material.

Like any work worthy of deeper study the notes are only of interest if a reader has first read the poem and enjoyed it even if the reader did not understand everything.

'Rivers'

The poem uses the various references in the red pill versus blue pill argument / philosophy to highlight the current imbalance in the mainstream media, where a storm of fake news and bias is all we can experience these days without reaching for more extreme and therefore dangerous outlets. How often do we ask, 'What is real and what isn't?' and can we even tell the difference anymore? The old order (conservative news bias) seems to have been replaced by a left-leaning, liberal, metropolitan elite who are far less tolerant of dissent, see diversity as a strength (even though many scientific studies have proved too much can be disadvantageous to a community), promote women and minorities over white, working class men and believe weakness (especially in terms of masculinity) is a virtue.

Yes, this is an anti-snowflake / anti-feminist poem and I make no apologies for this but I also hope that a reader might examine the philosophical literature, art, film and science contained within which I've used to highlight the problems in western culture at this crossroads in our history. It appears, once again, that the main players (we'll call them left-wing and right-wing for the sake of argument) can't compromise or meet half way but wish only to totally eliminate the other side. It's a very childish way to behave and can only result in disharmony and further conflict.

With the state of men's mental health very much in the news at the moment the battle between good and evil, right and wrong, light and dark is surely very topical even though the recurring theme in the poem might be one of mysticism.

Ultimately, what I'm asking is that we make a choice that benefits the planet and our place in it rather than continue along this narrow, selfish path to doom.

Line 1 - Daoist writer, Master Zhuang, once dreamed he was a butterfly. He didn't know that he was a man who had dreamt he was a butterfly, or a butterfly dreaming that he was Zhuang Zhou. This distinction is called the 'Transformation of Things'

Line 2 – 'ignorance is bliss' coined by English scholar and poet Thomas Gray / also a line from the film 'The Matrix'

Line 5 – Plato's 'Allegory of the Cave' (the beautiful prison)

Line 7 – 'curiouser and curiouser' from 'Alice in Wonderland' by Lewis Carroll

Line 9 – author Jake Horsley compared the red pill to LSD and describes the blue pill as addictive. In the film 'The Matrix' offers a series of choices between taking the blue pill or not. Habits and routines mean the people are dosing themselves with the blue pill

Line 10 – 'tessellate' is the first (of many) references to M. C. Escher, a Dutch artist whose work features many 'impossible objects' exploring infinity, symmetry and perspective. His work appears in Douglas Hofstadter's 1979 book 'Gödel, Escher, Bach'

Line 12 – 'Mesopotamia', site of one the earliest human civilisations from around 10,000 BC where it is thought humans first invented the wheel, planted cereal crops and developed cursive script, mathematics and astronomy.

Line 13 – humans have been compared to viruses (disease) invading all corners of the globe

Line 15 – from the Mock Turtle, 'Alice in Wonderland'

Line 16 – another line from 'The Matrix'

Line 17 – in the film, 'The Matrix', Neo's character lives in Room 101, which is taken from George Orwell's novel '1984'

Line 19 – 'Winston' is a character from Orwell's novel that hates rats. In the book 'The Ministry of Love' identifies, monitors, arrests, and converts real and imagined dissidents. In Winston's experience, the dissident is beaten and tortured, and, when near-broken, he is sent to Room 101 to face the worst thing in the world, until love for Big Brother and the Party replaces dissension.

What is also quite scary is that scientists in North Carolina and Brazil working with rats have actually achieved what the film 'The Matrix' implies and connected, via the Internet, the brains of two rats. These allow the rodents to share sensory information, collaborate on tasks to earn rewards, and fight back against the shadowy and cyber-apocalyptic forces that have enslaved them.

'A Brain-to-Brain Interface for Real-Time Sharing of Sensorimotor Information', Pais-Vieira, Lebedev, Kunicki, Wang & Nicolelis *Scientific Reports volume 3, Article number: 1319 (2013)*

Line 26 – 'up, up, up', from Escher's engravings

Line 28 – 'the god of dreams' is Morpheus (Greek mythology), who offers Neo the choice of pills in the film 'The Matrix'

Line 30 – 'two sweets' – the choice of pills, 'red' for brutal truth and knowledge, 'blue' for ignorance and an illusion of happiness. Cf. to the liquid ('Drink me') and cake ('Eat me') in Lewis Carroll's classic children's book

Line 31 – a loose reference to zoologist Chris Packham's 'Fingers in the Sparkle Jar', his memoir about his struggle with mental health issues

Line 33 – 'policewoman' – referring to the fact that women have taken over the world (in western democracies) and now dominate most top professions, including the media, which is instrumental in free-thought oppression. Cf. also to the 'red pill movement' (male rights)

Line 44 – 'Down, down, down…' – more Escher

Line 48 – 'stars' and 'snakes' – just two of the many Escher illustrations

Line 51 – 'Hobson' – refers to the 'take it or leave it' choice that Thomas Hobson, a stable owner with forty horses, gave to customers. Choose the horse nearest the door or none

Line 52 – 'sweating' – from the film 'Total Recall'. When Quaid saw a bead of sweat, he immediately knew that it was reality

Line 54 – '*say hello to your (my) little friend*' – from the film 'Scarface' (Al Pacino's character has finally gone over the edge)

Line 56 – the blue pill analogy in IT terms is malware (in the form of a 'rootkit') that sits on the operating system with full administrator privileges. The OS 'believes' it is real whilst the red pill (antivirus software) is used to detect and destroy the virus

Line 59 – 'evil demon' – imagined by Descartes to present a complete illusion of an external world: 'I shall think that the sky, the air, the earth, colours, shapes, sounds and all external things are merely the delusions of dreams which he has devised to ensnare my judgement.'

Line 66 – 'organ' – another reference to J. S. Bach who composed fugues with recurring themes

Line 69 – 'experience machine' – from Robert Nozick's 1974 book, which argues against ethical hedonism

Line 73 – 'Sanson' – Marie Antoinette's executioner

Line 74 – 'Gregory Four' – in the 13th Century Pope Gregory IV announced that black cats were instruments of Satan and should be exterminated. The result was a rise in plague-carrying rats

Line 76 – 'Hitler' – Adolf Hitler was nominated for the Nobel Peace Prize in 1939 by E.G.C. Brandt, a Swedish politician (although it was done as a joke)

Line 78 – 'muzzle that bitch' – in the 17th Century women who spoke out of turn were forced to wear a metal muzzle that locked around the head and sometimes included a spiked plate that would be placed in her mouth

Line 82 – 'cave dwellers', Plato again

Line 86 – 'cause', Brexit, 'wall', Trump (Mexico)

Line 90 – 'epsilon', from Aldous Huxley's 'Brave New World' (class system)

Line 93 – 'bricks', a reference to the selling of lumps of concrete from the Berlin wall (or not)

Line 101 – going off grid to escape mental breakdown

Line 105 – 'Dalmatians' – black and white (choice)

Line 125 – 'cured', 'beaten', 'cut' – the Men's Right Movement (MRM) campaign against discrimination against men e.g. family law, parenting, domestic violence, circumcision and mental health issues (suicides are higher amongst the male population) / also comparing men to meat

Line 127 – 'fair', has feminism gone too far? Two wrongs don't make a right

Line 128 – the course of a river is used as a metaphor for how things shift. A small change that isn't challenged soon becomes a rapid flow until it's too late to halt the forward motion

Line 140 – in the film 'The Matrix' it is the body heat / electricity of humans that is transferred as energy to the machines

Line 163 – making great experiences must be how we stay sane

'You and I'

Line 10 – 'gold' is a reference to Eldorado and the golden king

'River Wye Weekend'

Line 2 – folklore says there is a sleeping giant in Pumlumon

'Stranger in a Strange Land'

Line 4 – my uncle (Reg) used to think his son would one day achieve greatness

Line 6 – my cousin (Geoff) spent years living the genuine 'hippy' lifestyle doing all manner of amazing things

Line 11 – he was living in a flat in London when the serial killer Dennis Nilson was at large

Line 12 – my aunty (Gillian) inherited a fortune from her grandfather's businesses in the city, while her brother got nothing

Line 20 – my next contact via a Facebook message

Line 25 – 'grok' – from the 1961 sci-fi novel, 'Stranger in a Strange Land' by Robert A. Heinmlein where he coins the word 'grok' meaning to understand by empathy

Line 30 – 'blade' – sex change

'Egypt'

Line 2 – 'per ardua' (Latin) meaning 'through adversity' – the motto of the RAF Regiment

Line 5 – my father was in the RAF Regiment (known as The Rock Apes) and they were described as such whilst serving in North Africa

Line 13 – my father (a good swimmer) swam in the Suez Canal

Line 20 – the Muslim terrorists used to lay wire across the road, pulling it up quickly when a jeep passed to decapitate the officer who often stood up in the vehicle

Line 24 – it was terrible to see lung cancer take the strength away from my father

Line 28 – 'silver halide' used in photography

'Pills'

Line 1 – 'six million' is the approx. number of people taking antidepressants in the UK

Line 5 – 'blood tattoos' – self harming / 'Dylan print' – one of the artist's best loved albums is 'Blood on the Tracks' and one of his more well-known paintings is titled 'Train Tracks'

Line 12 – 'asparagus-coloured', Prozac (fluoxetine) the antidepressant drug is often green

'Half Empty Bed'

Line 10 – 'Mashed', from Barry MacSweeney's poem 'In With The Stasi'

Line 15 – 'Citalopram' (antidepressant drug)

'Scratching The Surface'

Line 3 – 'cool breeze' is from Tom Wolfe's 'The Electric Kool-Aid Acid Test'

Line 4 – 'Browns', the pub in Laugharne where the famous photograph of Dylan Thomas and Caitlin was taken

Line 8 – 'Tangled Up In Blue' (Bob Dylan), 'Dancing Barefoot' (Patti Smith) / Sir Gawain (St Govan) – King Arthur's nephew

'you came early'

Line 4 – 'Tom Petty', we made a mix tape to play for the hospital staff during my daughter's birth and Eve appeared as 'Into The Great Wide Open' was playing

'A Dream of Gawain'

Line 2 – the 'Penrose stairs' at St Govan's church are supposed to be magic because their number changes depending on whether you ascend or descend / Roger Penrose's impossible objects

Line 8 – 'Green Knight' from Arthurian legend

Line 9 – 'holy well' relates to the legends of the church bell and rock at low tide

Line 14 – 'Gringolet' was St Gawain's horse

Line 15 – "keincaled' means handsome and hardy in Welsh

'I Miss You'

Line 1 – my father started work on the railways at fourteen

Line 7 – 'Mallard' was a steam locomotive that broke the speed record in 1938. My father was the fireman on various trains that sped between London and Brighton (in the late 40s) and once shovelled thirteen tons of coal in a shift

Line 10 – 'Catterick' was the RAF Regiment base

Line 11 – my father was an accomplished marksman / sniper

Line 17 – 'Muslim Brotherhood' (the precursors of Al Qaeda who fought against the British in the 1950s)

Line 30 – floods in our street

Line 37 – my father was an electrician

Line 41 – 'tarantulas' – a school friend (Pies) and I worked in the textile factory when we were teenagers and were shocked to discover giant spiders, and even a snake, that were found crushed in the material that got shipped in to the factory from overseas

Line 59 – 'FAT' was a complicated card game that the men played down Cilfynydd Con Club

'Isolation'

Line 7 – 'cwtch' is Welsh for cuddle

'Cardiff'

Line 5 – the Marquis of Bute was responsible for much of the development of the city

Line 8 – 'zoot-zone' – Cardiff was a melting pot of races and cultures / the zoot suit was popular amongst young blacks around the 1930's

Line 11 – Cardiff has always been a very 'English' city, even though it is the capital of Wales

Line 13 – 'sugar' – many African Caribbean people arrived in Britain as slaves / cheap labour, transported by ships that housed imperial products, such as sugar, cotton, tea and rum

Line 19 – 'foreigner' (translation of the word 'Welsh'). Although Celtic-speaking peoples were living in Britain long before the arrival of the invaders from Friesland and Jutland it was the Celts and not the invaders who came to be called 'strangers' in Old English

Line 24 – 'Bucket of Blood' and 'Snakepit' – old pubs

Line 32 – 'James Bond singers' – Shirley Bassey was from Splott, Cardiff

Line 34 – 'tonality' – Cardiff in the old days was a truly multicultural city unlike today where we just see ghettos and monocultures

'For David Neville'

When I was in primary school in Cilfynydd one of our little friends (and his baby sister) were murdered by their father

'Christmas Dad'

Over Christmas (2018/2019) a local policeman (and ex-serviceman) hanged himself because of depression, something that is becoming more and more common these days

'Tết'

Line 1 – the uniform of the VC

Line 4 – the battle of Huế was one of the bloodiest of the whole American war

Line 10 – the soldier is inspired by the life of Ho Chi Minh whose life story is extraordinary

Line 25 – the Tết holiday is the most important celebration in the Vietnam calendar

'Somewhere near Barcelona'

Line 4 – porn actress

Line 22 – abused by her father

'Out of the Depth'

Line 2 – 'Little Boy' was the name of the atomic bomb dropped on Hiroshima

Line 15 – Saint Nicholas is the patron saint of sailors, merchants, archers, repentant thieves, children, brewers, pawnbrokers, and students in various cities and countries around Europe

Line 16 – 'albatross' – Cf. Coleridge's 'The Rime of the Ancient Mariner'

Line 22 – 'fuka' – Chinese shark fin soup is called fuka-hire (fin of fuka) in Japanese

Line 26 – a duppy is 'a spirit or ghost' that is usually bad. Jonah is the biblical prophet who lived in the belly of a whale

Line 27 – from Coleridge's great poem again

'Belle de Jour'

From the surrealist plot of the film of the same name starring Catherine Deneuve

Line 5 – 'sovegna vos a temps de ma dolor' – from Dante's Divine Comedy, roughly translated as 'at the appropriate time, recall my pain'

Line 14 – from T.S. Eliot's 'The Love Song of J. Alfred Prufrock'

'Porphyra'

Line 14 – Kathleen Mary Drew-Baker was a British phycologist, known for her research on the edible seaweed *Porphyra laciniata*, which led to a breakthrough for commercial cultivation. She was named 'Mother of the Sea' in Japan and there is a monument to her at the Sumiyoshi shrine in Uto, Kumamoto

'Bebe the Pomeranian made it to Lifeboat 7'

The last hours of the Titanic through the eyes of the dogs that survived the sinking. The menu items are from that fateful last supper

'Outlaw'

Line 23 – 'the next voice you hear' is from Jackson Browne's song of the same name. The escaped madman invents his own secret world to protect him from reality just as in the song the singer is saying we should choose our own path in life and not care about what other people may think. So I guess what I'm asking (as in 'Rivers') is who are the real crazy ones?

'European Tinder'

A play on words as the dating app 'Tinder' asks you to swipe one way or the other in order to make a choice. When Notre Dame burnt down the press / media were quick to assure us all that this was an accident even though they had no evidence of such! The reason for this swift denial was because many suspected it was an act of Islamic vandalism (as many thousands of Christian churches have been attacked, burnt or desecrated during the last few years throughout Europe). Yet another example of when the truth is irrelevant if it conflicts with a warped, liberal-left view of the world. The term 'brainwashing' comes from the Taoist religion and literally means to cleanse / wash the heart / mind

'Angelystor'

Is an ancient Yew tree in Llangernyw, Wales. The tree is at least 1500 years old but many people believe it to be almost 5000 years old!

Line 2 – I may have used artistic licence here as the Sumerians used cuneiform shapes almost 5500 years ago (Kish tablet)

Line 18 – Hywel Dda was king of Wales a thousand years ago

Line 24 – yew tree bark / needles are used in cancer treatment / chemotherapy drugs

Line 28 – the Amazon fires

'Cabinda'

Cabinda is a disputed exclave and coastal province in Angola

Line 1 – the Bakongo is the group name for several tribes from present day D.R. Congo / Angola who traded in slaves, first amongst themselves and then with the Portuguese

Line 5 – 'nzimbu shells' was the currency (shell money) of the Kongo peoples

Line 9 – 'Charleston' – the first port reached after crossing the Atlantic

'Laika'

The first animal (space dog) to orbit the earth. No plans were made to bring her back safely

Line 6 – 'kefir' – fermented milk drink popular in Russia

'Blade'

London knife crime

Line 2 – 'snow', pure cocaine has a floral smell

Other books by Dave Lewis:

Poetry:
Layer Cake © 2009
Urban Birdsong © 2010
Sawing Fallen Logs For Ladybird Houses © 2011
Haiku © 2012
Roadkill © 2013
Reclaiming the Beat © 2016
Going Off Grid © 2018
Never Seventeen © 2018

Novels:
Ctrl-Alt-Delete © 2011
Raising Skinny Elephants © 2013
iCommand © 2015

Edited:
Welsh Poetry Competition Anthology © 2011
Welsh Poetry Competition Anthology II © 2016

Non-Fiction:
Photography Composition © 2014
Land's End to John o' Groats © 2015
Wales Trails © 2016
Happy © 2017
Basic Photoshop © 2017
Hadrian's Cycleway & Coast 2 Coast © 2019

Websites:
www.david-lewis.co.uk
www.welshpoetry.co.uk
www.publishandprint.co.uk
www.wales-trails.co.uk
www.welshwriters.co.uk

Published by
www.publishandprint.co.uk

Printed in Great Britain
by Amazon

54565746R00063